Angels

in Connecticut

The simple truth about angels.

Susan Pettella

www.AngelsinCt.com

Susan Pettella
East Haven, CT
Please send all inquiries to:
angelsinct@yahoo.com

ISBN: 1453838295
ISBN-13: 9781453838297

Contents

Preface

I am not a famous author, nor am I an angel expert. I am just an average person on a journey to fulfill my life's purpose, and that is to share with you the truth about angels and all the joy they have to offer.

There have been many mountains in my path. I have suffered both physically and emotionally. And, I will admit that I have made many mistakes. And for all them, I am thankful as they have led me to where I am today. I realize that I could not have moved those mountains, survived the pain or learned from the mistakes without my angels who have always been with me offering guidance and protection.

Throughout my life I was given signs, had intuitions, gut feelings that I assumed were just coincidences. Now I know the truth. There are no coincidences in the universe, everything happens for a reason. And, once your eyes open to the truth, it can no longer be denied. Angels are here to offer guidance, to bring messages from God himself, and to show us the spiritual paths to follow.

Looking back at your own life, think about a time when you had a gut feeling about something or someone. When you followed your intuition and you made the right choice. Or, when you had that feeling and ignored it perhaps making the wrong decision. Have you ever thought about someone you haven't seen in a long time and then just happen to run into them? Or, have you ever got off the wrong exit or missed a turn in the road, and didn't know why? Did you just assume it was coincidence?

Many years ago when I was only 10, I would wake from a deep sleep every night at the same time. This went on for several nights. My mother gave me a book to keep on my nightstand so I would be able to read and eventually fall back to sleep. The nights continued with this pattern for more than a week until one night I woke up at the same time as I had been, only this night I was surrounded by smoke. I could smell it, see it – something was wrong! I ran to wake my parents, then my sisters. We all got out safely.

The fire had started in the clothes dryer. That night my mother had put a load of laundry in and set the timer, but the dryer never turned off and the clothes became so hot that they actually caught on fire. This was before the invention of smoke detectors so there was no alarm to alert us of the dangerous situation that surrounded us.

After that night, I slept soundly until morning. At the time it was considered a coincidence. Now that I am older and my eyes have been opened to the truth, I believe that it was a sign. I was giving the gift of saving myself and my family. It wasn't our time.

It was several years ago that I completely connected spiritually in body, mind and soul. Not through a specific religion but through the beauty I found in nature, in the blue sky, sunsets, the stars and the universe as a whole. It was a time of transition for me. After a not-so-pleasant divorce, although I don't know if there is such thing as a pleasant one, I decided to change careers. It happened fast and felt so right that it was more of a calling then a choice.

I was working as a graphic designer on a monthly newspaper, and was constantly under deadline and handling problems. I felt trapped in my office, in my life. I needed to do something to fulfill my life's purpose. I wanted to make a difference and find an inner-peace I so much desired. That's when I enrolled to become a licensed massage therapist.

At the time, I had been searching for answers to questions that I didn't even know how to ask. I was just wandering through life hoping to find peace, truth and love. I was just beginning to learn how to let go and open my mind to anything that lied ahead. I was on a journey, climbing mountains, and tackling my fears.

One of my favorite things to do was watch the sunset. I would go to the beach as much as possible just to sit and pray as the sun descended on the horizon. There I felt an inner-peace, a connection to my higher power. It sometimes brought me to the most wonderful tears of joy, cleansing my soul and overwhelming me with admiration for God. Then amazing things started to happen.

One December morning in 2005 something changed my life. It was cold and still a mess from the previous day's snow. My teacher was running late for our class. I stood in the front door of our school embracing the sun as it beamed directly through the glass. The warmth and light it delivered brought me instant joy, so much that I ran to get some classmates to share it with me.

During lunch break that same day, I parked my car in the upper lot at school. I was alone and there were no other cars in the lot. Looking up into the blue sky and sunshine, I smiled and took a deep breath allowing the peace to fill my body. Then through feathered clouds I witnessed the most beautiful rainbow. Every color was so vivid. One right after the other – red, then orange, followed by yellow, green, blue, and violet – it was like a slide show!

The day wasn't over yet. Just before retiring for the evening I went outside to once again look up at the sky. The clouds were thick but the moon shined through a perfect circle. There were rings of colored light surrounding the clouds that opened to let the moon through. Again, I watched in admiration as I thanked God and accepted the beauty of all His creations. I was in total peace, and love filled my heart. Just then a cloud floated through the circle – a cloud in the shape of a heart. I didn't know what to think, my mind just opened and within the clouds to the right of the moon I saw my God.

I say my God although I am not sure whose face it was. God. Jesus. Archangel Michael. I'm not sure, but there was a man's face perfectly etched in the clouds that night. Every detail of his beard, his eyes and lips were clear for me to see. It never crossed my mind to get a camera. I couldn't move. All I could do was welcome Him with unconditional love and without doubt or fear. It slowly faded but I will never forget it. Someone from above was watching over me. After that, I felt refreshed, opened, cleaned, awaken and peaceful. I had then, and still have, a general feeling that I am not alone. And, I will never be alone on this earth as my journey continues.

That day I was given answers to the questions I had never asked. I have not seen another rainbow slide show or the face in the clouds since that night, and I don't need to. I know that faith is just a matter of believing. To hear unspoken words, see the unseen, and follow the feeling in your heart for all that is good is one of the greatest gifts God has to offer us.

Introduction

Over the last several years I have become more aware of angels. I started reading about all the wonderful things they do for us. The miracles they perform and the guidance they offer even when we have not asked for it. And, when we do ask, well they are more than happy to assist us! As I talked openly about angels, I had many people relate stories to me about encounters and miracles that had touched their lives.

Honestly, at the time I was overwhelmed with projects, ideas, inventions, and working as a licensed massage therapist – I had no time to put together a book! Or, did I? Trying to make ends meet as a single mother in this poor economy, I prayed for guidance and strength to fulfill my life's purpose.

As always, I travel on my path staying open to signs that show me the right road to follow. And, when I'm unsure, I openly pray for guidance and ask for signs. I realize now that the right path is not always the easiest one to take. Sometimes it's the hardest path that is the most rewarding. Also, it's not about how much money you can make, because that which makes you rich in spirit has no price here on earth.

With this book I wanted to inspire people to believe and trust in angels by sharing true stories from ordinary people just like you and me. Not knowing where to begin, it remained in the back of my mind as I continued working on other projects. However, the angels had other plans for me. I was at a craft fair selling Peace Packs that I had handmade. It was there that I met two local authors and after talking for a brief period, I found myself traveling a different road. I was writing this book.

With the help of my angels, I have published this book. There were periods during the process when I became overwhelmed and unsure. During those times, I handed my worries and doubts over to them again asking for guidance and assistance. They have never failed me. As I said, angels are all around us just waiting to help each and every one of us – all we need to do is ask and believe. It's that simple.

In the pages that follow you will find more information about God's messengers and how you can invite them to be a part of your life. Included are stories from real people whose lives have been touched by angels, as well as photos, inspiring quotes, prayers and meditations.

I hope this book brings to you the inner-peace and spiritual belief you deserve to continue traveling peacefully on life's road. For that's my intention, my goal, and my life's purpose.

Acknowledgements

There are a few people I would like to thank in helping me complete this book.

First, I wish to express my gratitude to the many people who so generously contributed their stories and photos. You have made this book possible by sharing your personal experiences.

To my daughter Angela who allowed me to work past midnight and share the only computer we own in order for me to work on this book. Thank you for being the best daughter a mom could ever ask for. I love you!

To John, who encourages me to not only dream, but to believe in my dreams. Your faith has shown me first-hand how angels help us on our journey. Forever.

Thanks to my mother for proof-reading, my father for believing in me, and my two sisters for just being there for me throughout my life. And, a special thank you to my best friend Lisa for the many encouraging words and support.

Mostly, I thank all my angels who have brought me to this and through this. I believe and trust that you will guide me, every step of the way, as I continue my journey to fulfill my life's purpose.

Angels in Connecticut
is dedicated to my dear Uncle Bob.
You are now in Heaven singing and dancing
with God's angels. I love you always.

Part 1
The Simple Truth about Angels

Believers look up, take courage.
The angels are nearer than you think.
—Billy Graham

Messengers from Above

The word "angel" is derived from the ancient Greek *angelos*, meaning "messenger". Angels are indeed messengers of God. They have been in existence since the beginning of time. Like humans, angels were created by God. But they are not human at all and never have been. They are of higher knowledge, power and mobility than we. They are servants of God, not our servants, and certainly not meant to be worshipped.

Close your eyes for a moment and picture in your mind an angel. Just the thought brings peace, perhaps even a smile to your face. Most people visualize an angel as a beautiful winged being with a flowing robe surrounded by a glow of pure white light. That is what most painting, drawings, and statues show us. Perhaps that is their true appearance. But they can certainly transform into any size, shape and color they need to. They can relay a message with the help of a dragonfly, or offer comfort in the form of a bird.

They are both visible and invisible to the human eye. Sometimes you can just feel them as intuition, an insight. The truth is that they will take whatever form the visited person is willing to accept.

There are a few gifted humans who can actually communicate with angels. They see them and hear them. Most of us cannot. Our five senses are just not capable of experiencing these miraculous beings of God's eternal light and love. Angels are in constant motion. *They are everywhere.* If our earthly eyes were to see them, if our ears were to hear them, we would be unable to focus on our daily tasks.

We would become so preoccupied that we would lose sight of our purpose here on earth and daily tasks. But they *are* there just as the air we breathe.

Think about this. When we are born we take a breath of air and begin life. Throughout our time on earth we breathe in air, breathe in life. And in the end, when our journey here is over, we exhale our final breathe. Air surrounds us day and night. We take for granted that it will be there, and never doubt its existence. Air, like an angel, is not visible. We just know it's there for us. Most of us don't question where air comes from, how it happens. We just keep breathing. Now let's think about angels. There may not be an agreed upon explanation for angels. We may not be able to see or hear them, but we believe they exist. We trust that they are there for us just as the air we breathe. *And they are.*

Our fascination with angels continues to grow. Belief and trust in angels is growing even stronger as people awaken from the need for materialism, from greed and separation from God. We are beginning to take on responsibility personally as we become our own person and seek the truth of our existence. We are seeking spiritual assistance more and more.

By opening your heart and seeking the truth, it will be given to you. Simply ask your angels to offer you the opportunity to develop wisdom, strengthen self-understanding, and overcome any obstacles in your path. Then trust that your requests have been heard and will be answered. It is important to know that angels cannot interfere with our own freewill. When we call on them, we must do so from a place within ourselves. We must ask with unconditional love and trust whole-heartedly.

We all have choices. We can surround ourselves with positive or negative energy. By thinking positive no matter what situation we are in, we can and will have a positive outcome. Positive thoughts, emotions and words strengthen our energy fields attracting angelic light.

Everyone has heard the saying *life's a journey, not a destination.* It's on wall plaques and bumper stickers. People say it openly in conversation. Some see it, hear it and believe in it. It means to keep traveling. Live life to its fullest. Never settle for less than you deserve. Realize that you have a purpose on this earth. And, trust that your travels will deliver you not to a destination here on earth, but to your final destination – Heaven.

Take a break now from daily stresses, problems which cannot be solved at the moment, and life in the fast lane. Once you understand your purpose and invite angels into your life, everything will become clearer and easier. Yes, the problems will still be there. Some may seem unavoidable – poor health, debt, unemployment, depression, abuse – whatever it is, it's time to let it go.

Change is one of the hardest things to do. That is why people stay in miserable jobs or relationships. It's easy to give up, but so much more rewarding when you don't. Whenever I am going through anything that seems too difficult, I remember this saying:

The only time you fail is when you give up and stop trying.

This simple saying has helped me climb many mountains. Not only because I believe in myself, but because I believe in God and all the positive energy surrounding us on earth and in the universe. Faith does move mountains. And, faith and trust in God keeps us strong in body, mind and soul despite the mountains on life's road. Life is not always easy, but it can be less stressful if we ask for help.

Have you ever met someone who smiles all time, who always seems happy despite their stresses and problems? Usually it is a person who is able to let go and find an inner-peace and trust within their heart. You enjoy being in their company because they help you relax. You feel lighter, happier in their presence.

Now let's take a person who isn't talking unless they're complaining. You know the type, the ones that find the glass half (or completely) empty. They're not such a joy to be around. They seem to bring you down. You feel stressed, tired and drained when you're around them. The difference is the negative energy that surrounds them, and the disbelief and lack of trust in their hearts.

As I said, we all have choices: positive or negative; trust or disbelief; strength or weakness; peace or stress. It's that simple. And the choices we make determine our travels. We have freewill on earth. Free to make decisions. We have the ability to reason. However, we also have the option of asking for help from Above. We can turn negative energy into positive and bring love and joy into our lives. And, yes, all we need to do is ask.

If you believe that you are God's child and He has given you life, then you must also believe that you indeed have a purpose on this earth. We all have a gift to share and a reason to live. Now God would not give us this life with a purpose and not offer us help. He is a good and understanding being of light and love. He has not forgotten about us. In fact, He offers us countless angels to guide us. They are full of positive, white light pure and true. They sing praise as they await our call for help. For that is their purpose, to help us on our journey.

Seeing the Signs

Once you ask for help from the angels, you must let go and trust. It took me a long time to realize that answers don't always come immediately. Sometimes different paths need to be traveled in order to find the right road.

Let's compare life to a road map. Say you are in Connecticut and want to travel to Maine. You get a map and plan the routes you will follow to reach your ending point. Along the way you look for signs to direct you. You may even stop and enjoy the scenery, meeting and talking to people. You are traveling.

Now if you were to ask for guidance to fulfill your life's purpose and your ultimate destination is Heaven, then you must stay open to the signs along the way. Ask and you shall receive, but patience and trust are part of that process. Seeing signs, being open to your intuition and asking for help along the way are important.

Once your eyes open to the signs, you will see them more and more. They have always been there, but they are even clearer as your mind, body and soul open and welcome them into your life. I believe they will come if you allow them to. Just as angels appear in the form we will accept, the signs will come as well.

Some people request the help of an angel then start their car only to hear a song on the radio with the word angel in it. Some receive a phone call from a long-lost friend when they are in need of companionship. Then there are animals that come into our lives when we are sad and lonely. The signs are not flashing neon. They are simple.

Many unexplained things happened as I was writing this book. I did not overlook them as coincidence. To me, they were signs that I was on the right path. I met with Blaise Zullo in my Branford office. His story "Pennies from Heaven" is included in this book. After meeting with him, I went home and wrote his story. The very next day while getting into my car there was a penny on the driver's side seat. I smiled.

Another time I was waiting for a woman at a local donut shop. I did not know what her story was about, but she wanted to meet with me personally. As I waited, I began reading a book I had with me. There was a quote in it that I liked, *Matthew 7:7*. I wrote it in my notebook so I would remember to include it in this book. Just then, Lynn Riodan came in and told me how her son Matthew had died in a car accident. Her story "On the Wings on an Eagle" is included in this book as well.

So how do you know that you are on the right path? How do you see the signs? Just be open and aware of your surroundings. Listen to your intuition. Connect with nature and your surroundings. Don't just assume that when things happen they are coincidence. Everything does happen for a reason, if you allow it to. And, when you truly open your body, mind and soul to the higher power that surrounds you, then you will begin to see the bigger picture. You will see the signs and receive messages from God through His angels.

Guardian Angel Prayer

Angel of God, my guardian dear,
To whom His love commits me here;
Ever this day, be at my side,
To light and guard, to rule and guide.

Part 2
Letters

The following letters were submitted by people who wish
to share their personal experiences of seen and unseen divine
interventions. The name and town of the writer
is listed at the end of each letter.
All towns are in Connecticut except where noted.

*Coincidence is God's way
of performing a miracle anonymously.
—Unknown*

Connection of Spirit on the Seven Mile Bridge

In April of 2006, I went to see my middle child Geno in Marathon, Florida. He had been told he had approximately one year to live.

I live here in New England, but spoke to Geno weekly throughout his health ordeal. I was aware that he had many health problems during the past two years, but until I spoke to his Doctor, I wasn't aware of the limited time we had left together. Geno knew and accepted this, but, as his Mother I did have denial.

The Sunday I arrived we went to a boat show at the Seven Mile Bridge. Geno was quick to point out to me the spot he wanted to have his ashes dropped. Being in that state of denial, I asked him to please talk about something else. He insisted that I should know where he wanted to be and how it should take place. He asked that I please tell the rest of the family, and to honor he and his wife's wishes. I agreed.

Geno passed on September 16, 2006. This was the day after leaving the hospital in Miami. Our family had just spent an entire week at the hospital where a group of specialists had led us to believe he would do fine on his new treatment plan. Geno made the statement in the hospital he would not live to see his birthday on September 26th. I continually encouraged him to think positive, meanwhile I saw him grow weaker and weaker.

His wife made arrangements for a "Celebration of Life" on November 5th, and family came from all over the States to be part of it. She chose that date because of the full moon and it gave her the time she needed to get all in order. The dropping of the ashes that afternoon was in the Florida Keys. The law in the Keys states that a person has to be 15 miles out to drop ashes. The crematorium had put the ashes in a coral biodegradable shell. We hired two boats to take us out. I didn't feel I could go as the weather had turned so windy we had to walk with our backs to it. I stayed on the dock with the other family members.

The captain told us to drive from there to the Seven Mile Bridge, and we could watch them drop the ashes from there. I thought to myself, "How can I witness that 15 miles out?" At any rate we went.

We saw the boats coming like two dots to the right on the Gulf of Mexico. I felt disappointed for Geno, as his wishes were to be on the gulf side and they were headed under the bridge to the east side. As the boats came closer, they headed under the bridge and anchored. The captain decided to put the law aside and stay closer due to the weather.

Some time went by, and finally my granddaughter yelled that they had dropped the ashes. My daughter Sandy and eldest son Craig were on that boat. After a while they asked to take it out of the water because it didn't appear to be disintegrating (the container was supposed to disintegrate in 6 minutes.) The thought of it being washed to shore due to the weather was a major concern. As they removed it from the water in the net, they saw that is was disintegrating on the bottom.

They decided to place it back into the water. As they did, it literally turned on its side from the water weight, and danced across the water to the *exact* area that Geno had pointed to back in April. My granddaughter, Alecia, ran to the top of the bridge and watched. Just as it submerged, a sting ray swam over as if to seal it with a kiss. I thanked God for the wind, and the rain that led to Geno being granted his wish, and also thank God for the sting ray that blessed and kissed Geno farewell.

Spirit forces were at work here for all of us to witness that day. I feel the sting ray assisted Geno in his dance across the water, taking him to exact spot in that large body of water he had chosen to be laid to rest. The sting ray was there protecting him, and sealed his next dimension with a kiss. My interpretation is that Geno received his own personal soul stamp. Geno was a fishermen, he loved the Gulf of Mexico and wild life. It was the perfect gift.

September 26, 1960 – September 16, 2006
Geno will be missed always and loved by us all.

– Jessie Shippy
Woodbury
www.spiritguidelady.net

*All that I have seen
readies me to trust the Creator
for all I have not seen.*
—*Ralph Waldo Emerson*

Message Heals a Broken Heart

It was 2001 and I was head over heels in love with the man I had spent the past two years with. Sure we had our ups and downs, as many relationships do, but we were together and happy…so I thought.

One day, out of the clear blue sky, my boyfriend informed me that he wanted to take a break from our relationship. His excuse was that he needed time for himself and promised that he was not going anywhere. My love for him was so strong that I was willing to grant him the space he wished for.

About one month later, he moved to California to be with a woman he had met on the internet. The pain I felt in my broken heart was unbearable. It was like suffering a loss such as a death, but there was no funeral.

I became so distraught that I lost thirty pounds in one month. I did not realize that I was clinically depressed at that time. When a person is clinically depressed, they are not in the right state of mind for self-care or to distinguish that something is wrong with them. I began passing out from dehydration. One day I passed out in my bathroom and hit the back of my neck on the toilet bowl. I woke up on the bathroom floor shaking in a cold sweat and shivering. I remember getting up and drinking a lot of water, then I went to sleep.

The next few nights, I prayed for God to take me in my sleep. I did not want to suffer any longer from the pain I was feeling. My heart was broken. My body was weak. It was unbearable. On the fourth night of doing this I had a dream that saved my life. I call it a dream, but in all honesty it was more than that, it was real.

I felt myself get up and stand in front of my mirror just as I do every morning when I get ready for the day to begin. As I was fixing myself in the mirror I noticed the most beautiful angelic little girl sitting on the edge of my bed. I quickly turned around to see who it was sitting on my bed, but there was no one there. I heard a magical, soft-spoken voice say, "You won't see me. You have to look in the mirror." Again, I turned and looked into the mirror. There she was, sitting on my bed in a pretty laced white nightgown. I stood in awe admiring her shimmery golden skin and hair. She then proceeded to say, "If you need healing you must call on Saint Vincent three times." And then she was gone. She never said goodbye. I didn't see her leave. She was just gone.

The very next day I had a hair appointment. I was sitting in the chair getting my haircut as the details of my angel encounter entered my mind so vividly. I asked my hairdresser if he knew who Saint Vincent was. He said that Saint Vincent was the Saint for Healing.

After some research of my own, I discovered that Saint Vincent is the saint specifically for the broken hearted. That day, I gave all the glory to God. I cried with tears of gratefulness to the Lord, Saint Vincent and my little angel who was indeed my messenger.

I called on Saint Vincent three times, and many times thereafter, not only for myself but many others. I am not

ashamed in any way of the way that I acted during that
period in my life. I had asked God to take me in my sleep,
but He knew that my pain and suffering had taken over me,
and instead He rescued me. I was sent a little angel with a
message from above that filled me with love and hope, and
changed my life.

– *Catherine Scillia*
Hamden

Imagination
is more important than knowledge.
—Albert Einstein

An Angel in the Window

One day my granddaughter Gillian was staying at my house. She was only 5 months old at the time. I realized that I had a few pictures left on my camera before I could take the film out to be developed. This was the year 2000, and digital cameras were not popular at the time. I started snapping pictures of Gillian as she sat in her highchair.

Imagine my surprise when I opened the envelope containing the pictures and spotted an angel floating just above Gillian. It seemed to be just outside my sunroom window watching over her. Was it her guardian angel hanging out with us that day? There seems to be no logical explanation for it.

I truly believe that we are surrounded by angels every day. I guess on this particular day this angel wanted us to know she was there.

– *Adrienne Hopkins*
West Haven

*Keep on asking
and it will be given to you,
keep on seeking and you will find.*
—Matthew 7:7

The Comfort of a Grasshopper

When my mom died back in August of 2009 as a result of a traffic accident, my universe virtually exploded like a supernova. We had shared 44 years together as I had never married. She was my mom and my best friend, and the loss of her was so enormous that I continue to wonder how I made it to this point without her in my life.

My experience was in a sign that my mom was still with me when I noticed a very large grass-hopper on the vinyl siding next to my front door. This insect was all green and about 4 inches long. I had never seen something so large. The grasshopper stayed there throughout the whole time period – from the wake to the funeral. In fact, my aunt and sister also believed the same as I did. It was just a feeling that she was there with us. We all sensed this as my mom was so kind and protective of all God's creatures. What a perfect way to show that she was there with us! Somehow through the sight of this grasshopper we were given hope and strength to make it through this difficult time.

I checked near the door the next morning, after all the services were over, and it was gone. I truly believe that this unusually large insect was a sign that my mom was watching over me and my family who traveled from all parts of the country to attend the services.

– *Alison DeMaio*
Hamden

*Faith is telling a mountain
to move and being shocked only
when it doesn't.*
—Unknown

Pennies from Heaven

The year was 1995. I was recently divorced and looking for work to support myself and my children. I was a stone mason by trade. Unfortunately, there was not much work available at the time for a mason. Being a spiritual man I prayed to find work, anything to make a living.

I was offered a job as a grounds keeper at a University. It was a far fetch from being a stone mason, but I accepted. There were times when my friends, who were masons heading to work, would drive by and tease me as I swept the grounds and emptied trash. The days went on and turned into years.

On the outside, I smiled. Inside I was empty. I wanted to be more creative. I needed to use my skills as a mason to create buildings and structures. I prayed openly to Jesus as I swept the grounds.

One day as I was sweeping I noticed two men walking my way. At first glance, I thought to myself that they were salesmen and I tried to avoid them. That didn't help as they came directly up to me and introduced themselves. One wore a gray tweed jacket. He was tall and distinguished-looking and introduced himself as Peter. The other man, Joseph, was what I would consider cute in a warm sense. He wore khaki pants and a blue flannel shirt, about 50 years old with dark hair.

When they introduced themselves, I shook their hands and I immediately noticed that their hands were unusually warm. We began talking and I told them all about my current work as a grounds keeper and how I really wanted to work as a stone mason since that was my trade. Peter told me that he too was a stonemason for many years. He said that he has been watching me work and knows that I am a hard worker. I was told to continue praying to Jesus Christ and all would be ok. We said our goodbyes and I went back to sweeping. I looked up to see them again as they walked away, but they were already gone. It was as if they had disappeared! The grounds were open and they couldn't have gone far, but I scanned the grounds and found no one.

Within days of their visit, I was offered a position as a stonemason. Doing what I loved and almost doubling my salary! I thought about their visit again. I was told that I was being watched, but I had never seen them on the campus before. I was told to continue praying, but I hadn't mentioned that to them. I went searching to find them. As hard as I looked, I never saw them again.

I then asked for sign to confirm what I believed in my heart – that Peter and Joseph were really angels, messengers from God sent to me at my time of need. It was then that I started finding pennies. I found one embedded in a cement step when I was working. Another time I was looking at ornaments, there were about one hundred on display, I picked one up and under it was a penny. My daughter and I went hiking and just off the trail was a tree with a hollow. I looked inside and yes, there was a penny.

I am a blessed man. I know now that those two angels delivered a message, and I continue to receive confirmation of my belief in the pennies I find. Today, I am retired and no longer a stonemason. I now work as a volunteer at Hospice where I am happy to share my stories with many wonderful people.

– *Blaise Zullo*
West Haven

A Message of Hope

My 28-year-old son Dave died in a motorcycle crash in May 1997. The day after his burial, I sat on the outside steps of my home. My whole family was crumbling. I felt helpless.

I had given up drinking back in 1986 and stopped smoking in 1995. I had a few choices to comfort me during this time, so I just sat there thinking and praying, trying to cope with the loss of my son.

As I sat grieving, I felt two hands come down and touch both of my shoulders, and then a voice saying everything is going to be alright. The words were not spoken aloud, but I heard them loud and clear.

It gave me such strength that I still haven't drank or smoked and when anything seems to be overwhelming, I remember the touch on my shoulders and I know that everything will be alright.

I have retold this story to many people and I still get goose bumps every time.

– *Andrew Carangelo*
East Haven

*For he will command his angels concerning
you to guard you in all your ways; they
will lift you up in their hands,
so that you will not strike your
foot against a stone.
–Psalm 91:11-12*

An Angel in the Sky

It was a beautiful sunny day. There wasn't a cloud to be seen in the bluest of skies. I walked to the front door to look outside and take in the beauty of the day. Suddenly out of nowhere, a huge angel appeared. It covered most of the sky. She was perfectly etched out of these very thin clouds like a beautiful painting.

Stunned, I ran to get my mother who was in the kitchen doing dishes at the time. I yelled, "Mom, come to the front door, there is a huge angel in the sky!"

She came running with me, dish towel still in her hand. We both looked up into the sky but the angel was completely gone. I looked at my mother and said, "Mom, I saw an angel, I know I did!" She looked at me and responded, "That angel was meant just for you."

I remember feeling so happy and blessed for the gift I had received that day. I quickly went to get a piece of paper and I drew a picture of the beautiful angel I had seen in the sky.

That was over 20 years ago, and I carry that drawing with me to this day. I know my angel is with me now and will be with me forever.

– *Barbara Cusano*
East Haven

The best and most beautiful things in the world cannot be seen or even touched. They must be felt within the heart.
—Helen Keller

Touch of Heaven

I had a near death experience that I would like to share. I was involved in a horrible accident. The bus I was riding in was completely demolished in a head-on collision.

Just before the accident happened, I was sitting in my seat praying. Simply passing time as the bus continued on its route to my stop. Then the accident happened so quickly, I heard the crash and the next thing I remember is seeing a bright light. It was intense and bright, but unlike the sun, it didn't hurt my eyes.

I remember starring into the light and suddenly a deep, deep tunnel appeared. I felt overwhelmed by joy. I wanted to enter the tunnel and continue through it. Everything about it was just beautiful and peaceful. I just knew it was Heaven! But before I could enter the tunnel, I felt myself descending. I was going downward and could not reach the end of the tunnel.

I became conscience again to the world around me. I did not want to return to earth. But I guess it was not my time. My soul was returned to my body here on earth.

When I was taken off the bus, I looked up and noticed we were in front of a convalescent hospital that had a cross on the top of it. It read Roncalli, who was Pope John XXIII. He was an extraordinary and lovable pope. I felt as if I was being looked after. I was back on earth but welcomed by hope.

That day I suffered lacerations and cuts, but no broken bones. It was a miracle! This happened 20 years ago, but I remember every detail so clearly.

I do believe in angels and I do believe that God sends angels to help us.

– Barbara Korenchuk
(Town Withheld)

Our Highway Angel

My mother-in-law was recuperating from an eye operation. She lives in Wisconsin. Since we have a dog and would be gone for over 10 days, we decided to take our trusted motor home to visit her. We checked all the right things to get the motor home and ourselves ready for the 1800-mile trip.

We packed up our belongings, as well as Petey, our 3-year-old Westie. He was, and still is, a puppy in many ways. And, like all terriers, he can be a terror. He was not too happy traveling long days and sleeping in the camper. His idea of going for a ride was to get ice cream, then going directly home to enjoy it. This was no short trip down the road!

We were about half way through our wearisome journey when we experienced a flat tire. We were traveling on I-80 in Ohio. It was a very busy and dangerous highway. My husband pulled over to the side of the road to safety.

As my husband exited to see just what damage had occurred, Petey jumped out of the motor home and started running west-bound on I-80. No amount of calling, yelling or chasing would get him to turn around and come back. We were sure that he would be struck and killed by of one the trucks passing by!

Petey just kept running. He didn't even acknowledge us and would not turn around. At this point, I had nearly giving up all hope of ever reclaiming our dog. I looked up into the sky and prayed to God to help us. At almost the exact same time, a gentleman driving by pulled to the side of the very busy highway and got out of his car. He went around to the rear of his car and knelt down. Petey ran straight into his arms. When my husband finally caught up to Petey, he was still in the man's arms. The man simply said that he had seen the dog running and my husband chasing after him. He stopped because he was afraid that the dog would be struck and either injured or killed.

This man was an angel of mercy. He had placed his own life in danger to prevent Petey from being injured. He was an answer to my prayers. We thanked him profusely and tried to reward him. He refused all offers and went on his way.

Petey was back with us. The tire was fixed and the rest of the trip was uneventful and safe. We are forever thankful for our meeting with the highway angel on that harrowing day. We thank God for the miracle that had occurred.

– *Barbara Olson*
New Haven

The Delilah Dilemma

One cold January morning in 2002, our "angel" Delilah came into our lives. It was a twist of fate that could have easily been overlooked. My husband, Ernie, stopped by the New Haven Animal Shelter on his way to work to make a donation. They were raising money to help cover the costs of surgery for an abused dog there, and we wanted to make a contribution.

Not realizing the shelter didn't open until later in the morning, Ernie found the door locked and decided to leave. It was then that he heard the barking of a small dog. It seemed to be coming from outside the shelter. At first he thought he was wrong since all the dogs were supposed to be inside when the shelter was closed. Weren't they? He followed the barking and found a small puppy tied to the fence behind the shelter.

When he approached the puppy, he felt like it was saying, "Get me off this fence and into someplace warm…now!" He followed his instinct, untied the puppy and took her into his car. He warmed her under the heater and fed her some of his turkey and bacon sandwich. So much for getting to work on time that day! Ernie waited until the shelter opened. When it did, he brought the puppy inside and explained what had happened. He told the officers that he would talk to me about possibly adopting the puppy, and bring our 3 and 4 year old daughters in the next day to meet her.

Here's the dilemma. Ernie wanted a dog and was hopeful that I would want one too. But, I was still heartbroken over the death of our beloved first dog, Desi. After discussing this further, we both agreed that it was meant to be. Karma, coincidence, fate, whatever you want to call it, there was a reason Ernie found that puppy. We adopted her!

After the required ten day waiting period, Delilah came home to us with a bad case of kennel cough. It took six long weeks, three different antibiotics, and a whole lot of love to get her well. I spent so much time trying to get her better that I didn't even realize she was actually helping to heal my broken heart during the process.

Delilah got well and grew into an unusually intelligent and communicative dog that loves people and other dogs. She still speaks to us, or I should say demands certain things from us, like her Kong or a treat. And, when she thinks we are overly stern in reprimanding a child, she chimes right in with an appropriate admonition of the offending parent.

Delilah is so much a part of our family now that she accompanies us on trips to Bed & Breakfast inns, road races, and family functions. With her, I have learned to love again all the things I did with Desi. She became my hiking companion and my co-pilot in the car. When I look at her, I see the puppy that I so desperately needed to heal. Her soccer skills, greyhound-like running, and all around great disposition have changed our lives forever. We all smile when we see Delilah and we understand her barking demands. I have often considered Delilah my angel on earth sent by my other angel Desi who is now in Heaven.

Delilah has also grown with our children and feels the need to always know where they are and to protect them no matter what. She is very much a protector and a mother hen to our children. One winter Saturday morning, I found my youngest daughter, Lera, having a grand mal seizure. What I also found was Delilah standing over her licking her face. From that point on, Delilah became the chief protector of Lera.

When Lera was experiencing frequent seizures, Delilah would stay by her side, even propping her up as if trying to wake her from the seizure. We also noticed that she would sense a seizure before it happened and would stay even closer to Lera just prior.

Our daughter spent a great deal of the summer of 2009 in the hospital. She had numerous surgeries. We were told by the neurosurgeon to be very careful with dogs when we brought Lera home. As soon as I got Lera settled at home, I let Delilah in from the yard and she immediately licked Lera's head. Of course I never told the surgeon, I just believed that Delilah was helping her little girl heal. Lera never got an infection and we are sure it was just another blessing from above.

Delilah continues to be Lera's angel. She no longer has seizures. We know that the neurosurgeon worked a miracle, but also believe that Delilah's love, attention, and licking has truly healed our Lera. Her emotional support saved my life when all I wanted was my Desi back. She made me realize that there are many dogs in the world that need people as much as they need owners. She remains my angel and I am thankful everyday that my husband found her that cold winter morning.

– Carol Asprelli
Woodbridge

Someone is Watching Over You

It was that time of year, time to get rid of all the clutter. A local church was holding their annual tag sale and I decided to participate. It was a perfect way to help the church while getting rid of some unused items.

It was a cool sunny day in late summer. I set up quickly before the customers arrived. Many people stopped by my table seeking treasures. It was pretty busy at first, but then settled down after a while. It was then that a woman came walking over to my table. She didn't say anything and seemed to be a bit of a loner. She was at my table for a few minutes when suddenly a dragonfly landed on the back of her hand. The remarkable part was that it just stayed there.

I mentioned to her that I had never seen a dragonfly do this. As it stayed on her hand, I decided to try to touch it. It still didn't move. I looked at her and for some reason felt compelled to say, "You must have something going on in your life because someone is certainly watching over you." She looked startled when I said this and replied, "I just found out yesterday that I have cancer." I told her how sorry I was and since dragonflies spook very easily that I believed this was a sign that someone up there is letting her know that she would be okay. No sooner did I release those words did the dragonfly take off into the sky. This woman was so appreciative of my encouraging words.

As the weeks went by I mentioned my experience to someone. They told me about a book in the gift shop at the cancer center about a dragonfly. It tells the story of the passing dragonfly looking over the living water bugs in the pond, giving them all hope of everlasting life. I was so surprised to hear of this dragonfly story. I had never heard of it before.

I am not sure what made me say those words to a total stranger that day. And, I'm not sure why after I relayed this message did the dragonfly move on. As far as I'm concerned, this was not a coincidence. That message was supposed to be given to her. I believe the angels sent a message through the dragonfly, through my words, without me even knowing. All I know is that I will never forget how good I felt that day and how thankful I was to be a messenger.

– *Cheryl Velardi*
Northford

Carried On the Wings of an Angel

I am excited beyond words to share my encounter with an angel.

It was January 1999, a cold and dark night, almost black. I decided to take a run over to my friend Pam's house. Her husband was fighting cancer and was in the hospital. I felt the need to let her know I was thinking about both of them.

So off I ran with a bouquet of roses in hand. When I arrived at her house, no one was home. I left the roses on her door step and headed back home. As I was running, my foot went into a small hole in the road causing me to lose my balance. I fell and was absolutely unable to move my foot. I looked around but there was not a soul in sight, not one car on the road.

I lay in the road helpless and began praying. After several moments I felt like I was being lifted, as if someone was there carrying me. This feeling and extra strength I received at the time continued to my home, up the stairs, through the door and I was then placed on my living room carpet. I didn't question what had happened I simply accepted it as a blessing.

Last spring, I was standing in front of a clothing store. I heard someone call my name. A very tall woman approached me. She hugged me tenderly and went upon her way. Was it my angel? The one who carried me that night so long ago? I don't need an answer. I believe in my heart that it was.

– *Claire Small*
Orange

*When I do good, I feel good; when I do bad,
I feel bad, and that is my religion.*
—Abraham Lincoln

My Father, My Father

My father died at home in 1990 from lymphoma, a cancer that at the time was treatable but not curable. He was a good strong man who watched over our family throughout his life.

In October 2008, my mother was admitted to a hospital in New Haven. She underwent surgery for non-threatening medical issues. Since she was 87 years old at the time, she was sent to a rehabilitation center to gain her strength before returning home.

Now during this time, I was in a depressed state due to my own medical issues. I was at home worried about my mom, while trying to gain my own inner-strength to move forward in life. Sad and drained, I entered a room in my home and found my father's photo on the floor. This photo was in a bag in the closet, how did it get on the floor? I didn't care to know how, all I know is that I picked up his photo and began to pray. I asked God to please let my father watch over mom. We needed it now more than ever. It had been 18 years since dad's death, a long and trying road without his presence in our lives. As I prayed, I felt a comfort, a peace that I can't explain in words go through me from my head to my toes, my depression vanished and has not returned since.

Soon after this event, my sister Margaret and brother Frank went to visit my mother at the rehabilitation center. My mother told them that dad came to see her. My sister just thought mom was imagining this because of her dementia or the medications. She disregarded it and continued visiting with mom. Then one of the nurses came into the room. The nurse said to my sister, "I met your father today." My sister's heart skipped a beat. "That's impossible," Margaret replied, "My father died 18 years ago."

We then gathered as a family to find out the details. My family asked to speak with everyone on staff that had seen our dad. We were told that an older gentleman came in to visit with mom. He had on a beige jacket and was using a blue oxygen tank. Two nurses were in the lobby when my dad entered the facility and signed in. They remembered him because his oxygen tank was making an unusual noise. During the last part of dad's life, he used a blue oxygen tank, much like the one the nurses described.

We were told that he continued through the facility and went to visit our mom. He pulled out an old brown wallet which contained a piece of paper. It had the name of my mother's nurse, and a list of medications she was currently taking. He asked the nurse that she be taken off of these medications as they were making her weak and were not helping in her recovery. He then said his goodbyes to my mom and the nurses on staff and was gone.

The facility allowed us to view the surveillance tape. We were excited, but much to our surprise, the tape did not show our dad. However, it did show the nurses and they seemed to be looking at someone walking by, but there was no one there.

I will say that because of his visit, the doctor reviewed mom's medication and she was removed from several prescriptions. She began to recover quickly. My family and I have no doubt in our minds that our father came to visit my mom during that period. We didn't need to see him on that tape. We believed the nurses and staff at the facility who confirmed his visit. And, I believe that God answered my prayers. God may have sent an angel in the form of our father. Or, perhaps God allowed our father one last visit to help mom. We may never know the answer, but what we do know is that we were blessed with a miracle.

– *Cathie Cretella*
North Haven

*A believer sees more on his knees than
a philosopher sees on his tiptoes.*
—*Unknown*

My Son is in a Better Place, He is in Heaven

My 28-year-old son died when he hit a tree riding his motorcycle. It was Friday, May 23, 1997 at 6:30 p.m. That night, after returning home from the hospital, I called my friend Anne for comfort. I told her that we had lost Dave. She said that he was in a better place. I banged on the countertop and yelled out through my tears, "I need proof!"

After talking with Anne for what seemed like hours, I looked out the window and pleaded with God to give me proof that Dave was in a better place. I remember apologizing to God for not simply believing, but I needed proof that my son was with Him.

After a long weekend, I decided to go to the tree where the accident had happened. It was Monday morning at 5:30 a.m. As I walked across the street to the tree, a car stopped with two passengers. They asked me if I knew the boy who died there on Friday. I told them that he was my son. They introduced themselves as Jill and Tony and said they needed to talk to me.

They told me that on Friday they were just passing by when they saw a man lying in the sun. They thought he was sunning himself and continued on. But Jill had a gut feeling that something was wrong and told Tony to turn around and go back. When they returned they found the damaged motorcycle by the tree. Jill said that Dave was still warm and she held him while Tony went to call for help.

I stood there crying and thanking them for all they had done for Dave. I asked them to come to the wake which was being held the following day. I knew my family would want to meet them and thank them as well.

Tony said that he didn't know if Jill could attend because she had back-to-back heart attacks recently and he almost lost her. She told me that her heart had stopped during the attacks and that she remembered seeing the doctors working on her as she went up towards a light. She kept saying she needed to go back because she still had things to do. She told me that she could see an amazingly beautiful place as she was going up through the tunnel towards the light. She had what is known as a near death experience.

As I drove away I realized that was the proof I had asked God for! Anyone could have found Dave that day. But by the grace of God it was a person who had a near death experience. She was the only one who could have given me that proof. I truly believe she was an angel sent to tell me that Dave is indeed in a better, beautiful place.

– *Claudia Carangelo*
East Haven

Catch Me When I Fall

I have always believed that angels surrounded us, that they watched over and protected us. However, one day after a strange encounter, my belief became even stronger.

My mother, a dear lady and in her own right truly an angel on earth. We were close as mother and daughter. My son was always close to his grandmother as well.

One day, a year after my mother had passed away I was heading downstairs to do laundry. Preoccupied with my laundry basket in hand, I tripped on the top stair and felt myself falling head first. There was nothing to grab onto. I was falling. Suddenly I was lifted straight up and placed down on a step. My arms then grabbed onto the rail and I was standing. I stood there, shocked and a little scared, wondering what had just happened. At the bottom of the stairs sat the clothes basket and my slippers. I immediately glanced at the photo of my mom that I kept downstairs. It was like she was staring at me. From that moment on, I knew that I had an angel encounter.

My mother was watching me that day and had angels sent to me to save me from a bad fall. Now I feel her watching over me where I go. She is still protecting me, as well as my son, as she did in her life on earth.

I believe that there are angels watching over all of us, and they are there to help us in many ways.

– *Darlene Anderson*
Hamden

*If you judge people, you have no
time to love them.*
—Mother Theresa

They Are Watching Over Me

There have been many occasions where I know that angels were guiding me and helping me through life's challenges.

The first time was in 1995, when I was pregnant with my oldest son, Travis. During the pregnancy we found out that he had Down Syndrome and a heart defect. I was scared and unsure what to expect and worried if he would be okay when he was born.

The day of delivery arrived. My water broke early that morning and we headed to the hospital. I assumed that I would be in labor all day and deliver the following day. However, the doctors said they had to induce me as soon as possible as they were concerned about my baby's heart and the possibility of needing immediate surgery.

The beginning part of this went well, but as the day wore on I became tired. When it came time to push they actually put me in the operating room as a safeguard. I was exhausted and felt like I had no more strength when I suddenly felt hands inside helping guide him out. I saw people from my life watching me and encouraging me that everything would be alright. I saw my grandfather, whom I had never met. I saw my great aunt, my favorite cats, and other family members that I could not identify. I just felt this sense of calm in the midst of a difficult situation.

Travis was born. He was blue. The umbilical cord had been wrapped and knotted, yet I did not panic, and less than a minute later I heard him cry. I really feel that during the delivery I was accompanied, not only by family members who have passed on, but by angels. Our angels watched over us that day and continue to guide us daily.

My second experience occurred in 2004. My best friend of over 20 years died of a brain tumor. Tisa had a heart of gold and was just the sweetest person that I have ever met. Her passing completely floored me. I had not known how serious her illness was.

The night after she passed I was at home spending time with her family and friends. There was gust of wind and the curtain formed a shape – her shape! It was like she was saying hello. I was not scared but rather comforted that she was not going to totally leave us. That she was okay.

The following day I needed to register my car. When I got to motor vehicles I found out that I needed to have the car that I was registering with me for an inspection. I was running short for time so I raced home to get the car. It wouldn't start. I asked her to help me, I turned the ignition again and it started. I would have thought it was just my imagination except for the fact that I actually felt her presence.

The day of her wake arrived. I was so upset. I didn't even want to go inside the building. I didn't want to say good-bye. I openly asked her for a sign that things would be okay. I immediately felt a breeze on my face and I knew she was there. I promised her that I would watch over her children, and I do to this day.

I have seen her presence in the form of butterflies and dragonflies. I know that she will always be looking over our shoulders. I talk to her often and ask her for guidance and I know that she listens to me.

I have had other things happen to me over the years, but it was not until these events occurred that I firmly believed there are angels amongst us all the time.

– Debra Giordano
East Haven

*If you conquer, you will be clothed like
them in white robes and I will not blot
your names out of the Book of Life; but I
will confess your name before My Father
and before his angels.*

—Rev. 3:5

Angels to Comfort and Protect

It was a warm September night. My son and I were driving on North High Street in East Haven heading to a toy store. I noticed headlights on the other side of road and slowed my vehicle down. There had been a motorcycle accident. It had apparently just happened since there were no rescue workers on the scene yet. There was only one car pulled over and a few people standing by. I saw the motorcycle on the ground and a man lying near it. I wanted to get out and help, but I had my son with me.

As I was passing by I made the sign of the cross and looked directly into the eyes of a young woman who was kneeling beside the man. She was comforting him. I called 911 but they had already received the call for help. A minute later I passed the fire truck heading to the scene.

The next day, I read about the accident in the newspaper. I learned that it was the brother of someone my sister went to school with. It was Luanne's brother!

Two years later, I was at the Town Hall paying my car taxes and I ran into her. I asked about her brother and explained that I was at the scene just moments after it had happened. She asked me if I remember seeing someone with him that night. I told her about the young woman kneeling beside him. Luanne said that her family heard about it and wanted to thank her, but that no one knew who she was. She seemed to have disappeared just after the rescue workers arrived. I believe she was an angel sent to comfort him until help arrived.

Another experience I had was when my son was five. I was sound asleep and he was sleeping next to me. I was suddenly wide awake, not by anything I can remember, I just woke up. I looked to the foot of my bed and I saw a woman standing there. She had dark black shoulder-length hair and a very pretty face. I looked into her blue eyes, but I wasn't afraid. I was calm and at peace around her. She wore a red silk blouse and black pants. Looking directly at me, she slowly ran her hand over my son who was still asleep next to me. She put her finger to her lips as if to say quiet, then she disappeared. I was left with such a peaceful feeling.

It has been over 10 years since her visit, but I can honestly say that I remember every detail and still feel at peace when I think of her. I am not sure if she is my son's guardian angel or mine. Either way she was letting me know that we are protected and she is with us.

– *Denise Tartaglia*
Wallingford

The Right Decision

God sent me an angel 12 years ago. My husband had dementia for many years. During that time, I took care of him. That involved changing diapers, feeding him, bathing him. Basically, all the duties and attention you would give to an infant. I quit my job and tended to my husband.

As time went on, our savings began to dwindle. I didn't know what to do. We had built the house we lived in and we loved it. It was our home and I just couldn't lose it. I needed a plan. I had to do something, but I did not know what the right decision was.

One night I was awakened from my sleep. My eyes focused to see the most beautiful angel directly above my bed. She waved what resembled a wand over me, smiled and then disappeared. After that I immediately knew what I had to do. It was time to put my husband in a nursing home. If I didn't, I would either lose everything or become sick myself. The very next week I enrolled him at Masonic.

It was then that I joined First Congregational Church in Cheshire. The support and welcoming I received from this House of God was overwhelming! With my husband safely at Masonic, I now had time to contribute to the Church. I began mentoring confirmation girls, baking cakes for coffee time, and was even elected a Deacon!

I knew I had made the right decision, not only for my husband, but for myself and the many wonderful friends I have made at the Church. All of this had happened because God sent an angel to visit me and offer guidance. And although there were no words spoken to me, I knew in my heart what had to be done.

Before, if anyone had told me this happened to them, I would not have believed. Now I would. Now I know the truth. Angels do exist.

– Dolores Bozzuto
Wallingford

A Glimpse of True Spirit Life

It was 1933 and I was a senior at Elmira College. I had an experience while studying astronomy that I will never forget.

One dark night my classmates and I stood on the flat roof of one of the dorms, taking time to observe the evening stars. Being astronomy students we were fascinated with the stars, planets, comets, and galaxies, and the universe as a whole. So absorbed in the vast universe above, I wandered off to be by myself in a dark corner on the roof. That night, not only did I see stars, I witnessed a sight that I have never forgotten.

A form appeared from the waist up. It was about 30 feet tall. It developed slowly and moved from right to left, lasting about 10 seconds before it disappeared. I just stood there in complete fascination. At the time I did not mention this to anyone although I knew what I saw was real. It was a wonderful experience!

Another time in my life I witnessed spirit life is when I was in Ireland. I was walking through an exquisite garden admiring my surroundings when something moved very quickly through some leaves and flowers. It startled me and caught my attention. There among the flowers, I noticed a very small green face looking up at me. It disappeared as suddenly as it had appeared.

These were two mysterious moments in my life that I shall never forget. I do believe that true spirit life surrounds us all, and sometimes we are blessed to get a glimpse of it.

– *Elinor Smith*
New Haven

Faith furnishes prayer with wings, without which it cannot soar to heaven.
—St. John Climacus

Flying with an Angel

I am here from South Carolina visiting my son in Connecticut. I happened to see your interesting request to send stories of angels. It so much intrigued me that I had to share my story!

Once, while flying from Hawaii to New Zealand, I saw something I will never forget. I had a window seat and was looking into the black sky as we flew high above the earth. Suddenly a face appeared at the window. It was round and smiling. It gazed at me for a few seconds then disappeared.

It was not my reflection. My companion was asleep beside me so did not see it. To this day I shall never forget that angelic face in the window. Although I cannot explain who or what it was exactly, I can say that it was there and it was real.

– *France Smith*
Newbury, SC

Remember to welcome strangers, because some who have done this have welcomed angels without knowing it.
—Heb. 13:2-3

The Hummingbird

Almost everyone appreciates gifts on their birthday. Some receive new clothes, jewelry, tickets to special events or perhaps flowers. However, my special birthday gift was ethereal, a true gift from Heaven.

It had been years since I've seen a hummingbird flitting around my yellow and red honeysuckle vine. Seeing them always brings instant joy to my heart. The joy is fleeting, however, because they usually disappear as fast as they come.

It was early morning in September, my birthday. I stood at my front window taking the bounty of flowers and trees in the front yard. Then, I noticed there was a hummingbird at the honeysuckle vine. He flitted from flower to flower getting his fill of nectar and filling my heart with joy. It then disappeared and I accepted its visit as a gift. I received an extraordinary birthday present!

My mom had passed away many years ago. She was also a lover of flowers and nature. Was this a gift from her? I believe it was and I accepted it as a gift of solace in knowing everything will be fine and that she is watching over me.

I have received many gifts in my life, but none as special and memorable as the visit of a hummingbird on my birthday. This, I will treasure forever.

– Jaci Dahlmeyer
East Haven

One life is all we have and we live it as we believe in living it. But to sacrifice what you are and to live without belief, that is a fate more terrible than dying.
—Joan of Arc

Fly and Be Free, For You are With Us

My son Anthony died in a car accident in August of 2002. He was only 19. My family has had many encounters with him throughout the years. It is a very long story, but in short he appears as a dragonfly and it is usually when we need reassurance the most. I have so many stories I could relate, this is just one.

It was the year after my son had passed and my mother decided she was going to bring her three youngest granddaughters to visit their Uncle in Las Vegas. My daughter, Theresa 12, was to go with her. I reluctantly agreed. Needless to say, I was still trying to cope with the loss of my son and liked my two daughters around. I needed to know where they were at all times or I would just about lose it.

The day came for Theresa to board the plane. They were flying out of Tweed New Haven. It was a warm July day, and we were standing by the fence watching them board. I stood there with my husband and sisters, waving to her through the fence as tears were streaming down my face. Then the plane started to move and get into position for takeoff. By this time I was all but hysterical. I prayed to myself, son please fly with your sister and make sure she is safe, I couldn't bear it if I was to lose her also.

I then started to lose it and insisted my husband go and stop the plane. She can't go. I don't want her to go! Stop holding me! Go and get her I screamed. As my husband was holding me, and trying to console me, a dragonfly flew between our faces. We were just inches from each other and it flew between us. Immediately I felt a complete calm come over me. I knew my son was telling me that Theresa was going to be okay. They all agreed that it was for sure his way of telling me to Chill Mom, she'll be fine and I am with her. And, yes, she was fine and enjoyed the trip.

– Janet Moscato
East Haven

Thursday Won't Be That Bad, I Promise

None of us thought we would be here; no one wants to be here.

I look around, I feel sorry for the boy with the face mask; probably leukemia. I see an infant with a large head and small body. I wonder what is wrong with her. Both her parents coddle and feed her. She is loved.

Then I realize that we too are here. Tristan, our Tristan, you cannot see his illness. How could this have happened to him, to us? My question falls upon deaf ears.

My heart aches for all of the sick children, but it breaks from my sick child.

This was written for all of the mothers who are everyday angels to their sick children. The title comes from the boy wearing the face mask. As the small build ten year old boy was being carried out of the doctor's office, in his mother's arms, she softly said, "Thursday won't be that bad, I promise." Her words broke my heart and inspired my writing.

– Joann Peterson
New Haven

*The way to see by Faith is to shut
the Eye of Reason.*
—Benjamin Franklin

Our Lady Came to Fatima

It was September of 1996, and I was working as a 911 dispatcher for the Town of East Haven. I was working the day shift at the Fire Department on Main Street when there was a knock on the door. It was a young nun dressed in a habit. She was about as tall as I am, 5' 2", she was slim and had the face of a porcelain doll. In her hand she held a book entitled *Our Lady Came to Fatima.*

She was selling it, but unfortunately I didn't have any cash on me to purchase the book. We talked for a while about the weather and how warm it was that day. I mentioned to her that as a young girl, I played Jacinta, the youngest child that was visited by the Blessed Mother, in a school play. I also noted how unusual it was to see a young nun in the traditional habit walking along Main Street. She then left and I continued working.

An hour later, there was a knock at the door again. It was the same nun. She said she had to come back to see me as I appeared troubled and sad and she wanted to give me the book. I explained to her that my son had passed away six weeks earlier. She asked me his name and I told her Daniel (I seldom referred to him as Daniel, but as Danny). She told me she would pray for me on his "name day". I asked when that was and she told me July 21st. I was amazed as this was the day that my son went into a coma at the age of 24. I literally could not speak another word. She turned and left. The door swung closed and I looked in the screen that was in the dispatch office, but never saw her leave the building.

When I got home I checked in a prayer book and she was correct about the name day. My son was 17 years old when he was involved in a car accident and he was paralyzed from the shoulders down. My ex-husband and I cared for him at home for 7 years until he was given drugs that were prescribed for a person who had a high insulin level. As a result he went into a coma and remained that way for 11 days. We, according to his wishes from an earlier conversation, removed him from all life support.

For the first time in 7 years, he clutched my hand, smiled and then left this world. I have felt his presence many times in the last 13 years and believe that he is now with the angels and has helped myself and others through some of the most trying times.

I do believe that angels surround us, protect us and help us to understand some of the unexplainable things that occur. I'm retired now, have two beautiful daughters and five grandchildren. We talk often of their Uncle Danny and two grandchildren have had encounters with him, although none knew him.

– Joanne Acabbo
East Haven

Circles of Angels

Over the last two years, I have had several experiences with angels.

It was Easter Sunday and my family attended church services to celebrate the resurrection of Jesus. After mass my son took pictures of his children on the altar. After he developed the film, he noticed there were circles over my grandson's head. They were also above two other children and scattered about in the photo. He just assumed they were just wet spots on his lens. The following month I attended a workshop about Angels. It was then that I learned that the "circles" were actually angels, spirits from above.

Another experience I had was when my husband and I attended a funeral. Our long time friend had passed away and his funeral was being held at the parish he belonged to. He was the one who built the altar at this church. What a beautiful job he had done! "Amazing Grace" played on the organ as the parish sang along through tears for our dearly departed friend. When the song ended and silence filled the church, I looked up at the altar and on the back wall floated circles – there were six of them floating from right to left. Without hesitation, I said out loud, "The Angels are here for our friend."

When my father was dying in the hospital, my brother and I were standing at each side of the bed. All of a sudden, my father looked straight upward and reached his hands forward as to grab onto something he was seeing. He told us that it was snowing. I knew in my heart that what he saw and described as snow, was actually his angel coming to take him to Heaven.

The angels have helped and guided me throughout my life. Over the past two years, angels have touched my life and made me a better person by opening my eyes and heart to their presence.

– Judy Damberg
Branford

Safely Up to Heaven

I have had several encounters with what I believe to have been angels in dreams, signs and visions. I would like to share my most amazing one with you.

In 2006, my dad was in Hospice with terminal cancer. He spent four weeks there and we visited every day. My dog would accompany us there and sometimes we would let him walk around visiting other patients.

The nurses would tell the families when their loved ones were close to passing so that the families would be prepared. My dad was not at that point yet.

One night my son and I, along with our dog, were visiting my dad. He was asleep. It was in the evening and I had been there for quite some time sitting on a very hard, uncomfortable chair. I was about to get ready to leave when my dad got a little restless. At the same time, my dog came running into the room and jumped up on a lounge chair. He put his head between his legs and looked up at me. I thought it was odd, but didn't think much about it as I was more concerned about my dad at the time.

The nurse soon came into the room and gave him a sleeping pill. At that very moment, I turned my back to my dad who was now lying peacefully and I started to pull the chair closer to his bed so I could sit for a while longer. As I was pulling the chair, I felt the most unbelievable sensation of something entering my lower back and then exiting through my chest in an upward movement. I asked the nurse, "Did my father just die?" I didn't look at him. The room had a clean feeling to it, almost like I was somewhere else and all alone. I just remained hunched over and frozen and then the nurse replied, "Yes he did."

I believe what I felt was the angel who came to get him. It gave me a sense of peace at the worst time in my life. Losing my dad was difficult to accept, but at the same time I felt comforted to know that his spirit, as well as all our spirits do go somewhere and I know for sure that they go upward. I was left in awe at what transpired that evening. I know that my dad was taken up to Heaven on the wings of an angel.

– Karen Carrano
Orange

A Message through a Child

Last year, my doctor informed me that I needed to have a minor surgery to remove a small polyp. Since I had never been under anesthesia, I had a lot of apprehension. I was afraid the doctor would find cancer, afraid that she would need to remove more than just the polyp, and even worried about not waking up afterwards.

As a teacher, I tried very hard to hide my feelings from my class. On the morning before my procedure, I was reading a book entitled *Teeth* by Joy Cowley to my kindergarten students during Readers' Workshop. The book was mainly about a variety of animals and how they use their teeth.

Right in the middle of my lesson, Leonel, one of my students, called out "Miss Karen, have you ever seen the movie *Fireproof?*" Frustrated that he wasn't paying attention, I asked him, "Why did you ask me that? What connection did you make between the movie and our story?" His answer shocked me.

He told me that he had to ask me and he didn't know why. I asked him what the movie was about. He answered, "In the movie, the firefighter was so scared, but he knew he would be okay because the Lord was with him." At that moment, all of my fears and anxiety left me. I knew that God was talking to me through this young man. He was and still is an angel in my life and will never be forgotten.

– *Karen McMahon*
North Branford

Faith is to believe what we do not see, and the reward of faith is to see what we believe.
—Saint Augustine

Seeing the Signs

A friend of mine called as I was running out the door to an appointment. I asked for her number so I could call her back. Hurriedly, I opened my dresser drawer and pulled out what I thought was a blank piece of paper. I wrote down her number and put it aside.

That day, my husband was told by his doctor that he was to report to the hospital the next week for a heart operation. Needless to say, I was worried about my husband.

That evening, when I went to call my friend back, I noticed that the paper I wrote her number on wasn't blank after all. On the other side was a Novena to Saint Joseph. I immediately thought that this would be perfect to say for my husband.

The day came and we arrived at the hospital as instructed. While he was in the operating room I went to the hospital chapel to pray. As I knelt down to pray, I noticed the Sunday bulletin next to me in the pew. It had been left there from the prior days services. Low and behold, I looked down and discovered in the bulletin that this very day was Saint Joseph's day. At that very moment, I knew that my husband would be fine.

After leaving the hospital, I went directly to a Catholic store and purchased a statue with the Novena of St. Joseph. I had it blessed and it remains on my husband's dresser watching over him. I do believe that my Guardian Angel helped me find that piece of paper with St. Joseph's Novena.

At a different time in my life, I had another angel experience. I had an elderly aunt who had never married. She was a very independent woman and lived alone most of her life. She became very sick as she aged, but wanted to remain in her home rather than be put into convalescent care. My cousins and I agreed it would be best to let her live the rest of her life at home with the help of a live-in companion to assist her.

One day I went to visit her. The companion and my aunt told me they were both bored. Out of the blue I suggested that they say the rosary together. The very next day my aunt passed away.

Two weeks later, one of my cousins and I moved one of my aunt's dressers in her bedroom. I looked down and discovered that underneath the dresser was the most beautiful pin of the Blessed Mother. I knew right then that she had arrived into Heaven and was with Mary. Again, my Guardian Angel was giving me a sign.

I believe there are angels among us, but a person has to truly have complete faith in God to allow miracles and angels into their lives.

– *Leslie Keeler*
Seymou

The Star Closest to the Moon

Every Mother's Day my husband Kenny would create a peaceful area in our yard. It was a gift of flowers and beauty just for me.

In one spot on a hill he placed an old barrel tipped on its side with flowers cascading as if they were tumbling down the hill. In another area, he placed a park bench and built a stone flower bed. It was here that he planted at least 20 daffodil bulbs. The first spring, only four daffodils came up. When I asked him what had happened, he laughed and replied, "That's cool, one for each of us!" He was referring to himself, me and our two children.

Spring turned into summer and before we knew it fall arrived. That winter, Kenny died. He was only 36 years old. I was in shock and my sadness was overwhelming. Kenny had always told me that I was a great mom. He used to say that we were an incredible team and together we could do anything. Now, I was alone. It was just me and my children and I missed him every minute of every day.

A few weeks after Kenny died I still couldn't get my daughter Jessica to go to the cemetery. She kept saying, "Daddy isn't there, he is in Heaven." I was afraid that she was unable to face the reality of his death and was determined to take her there. I had bought an eternal light for his grave and told her I wanted her to see how nice it looked. So we drove to the cemetery one night in December.

When we arrived, she simply said, "That's nice, Mommy." Then she ran around the cemetery in the snow avoiding the graveside. I was feeling as though I had failed to achieve what I had set out to do here with my daughter. I prayed and asked Kenny to help me. Tears ran down my face as I recalled how proud he was of our children. At that particular moment I felt lost. How would I do this alone?

Just then Jessica yelled, "Hey Mom, there is Daddy's star!" Thinking how sweet she was I turned and look up at the sky. I asked her how she knew which star was her dads. She replied, "That's easy. It's the one closest to the moon that way we can always find it." My tears returned again as I recalled Kenny's words to me over ten years prior, before Jessica was born.

Kenny was flying to Texas to visit his brother. One night prior to his departure, we stood outside under a star-filled sky. It was then that he told me not to worry. He said whenever I missed him or felt sad I should just look at that star. What star I asked him, there were so many. He pointed and said, "The one closest to the moon, do you see it?"

Again, I cried, but now my tears were filled with joy. My eight year old daughter wasn't born when Kenny said those words to me and yet somehow she knew. It was no coincidence. As we walked back to the car I noticed a message in the snow. It read: I Love You Dad, RJ. It was a message from my son who had visited earlier that day. I knew then that Kenny was still with us, and we were still a great team!

The winter passed and spring arrived. Still filled with loss and sadness, I wandered over to sit on the park bench in my yard. This was the peaceful spot that Kenny had built just for me.

But I felt no peace as I found myself shaking my head and crying out, "No!" I was still in denial and missed my husband tremendously. Then I looked up and in the flower bed I saw in full bloom – three daffodils! Remembering his words, I heard his laughter and found the strength to continue on. I thanked him and I thanked God for the time Kenny and I had shared together.

– *Lori Ann Toner*
Madison

For with God nothing shall be impossible.
–Luke 1:37

On the Wings of an Eagle

My son Matthew died in a violent car accident on May 23, 2009 while driving on Totoket Road in North Branford. He was only 18, a senior in High School and was only weeks away from graduating. Matt was very special. He was a loving son, loyal friend and a perfect brother to his sisters Elise, Alexa and Mea.

I had a very uneasy feeling about Matt the day he died. So much so that I told my daughter Elise that I felt bad for him. She asked why, but I couldn't put my finger on it, so I simply said I don't know.

It was a beautiful spring day. It was 70 degrees outside and gorgeous. That morning Matt did a lot of chores. He showered and we had a nice talk about a variety of different things before he pulled out of our driveway at 1:15 p.m.

While gardening, I heard sirens. It was 2 p.m. I can't explain it but I knew something had happened to Matt. I called him, no answer. I sent him a text "you okay?" No response. Very shortly after hearing the sirens a Detective came to my house. He had the horrible job of delivering the news of the accident to me and my family. Unfortunately, for him, he also had to witness the devastation on Totoket Road.

My husband was shouting for me, "Lynn we have to go, Matt's been in an accident." I ran to the front of the house, grabbed the Detective by his shirt and asked him if my son was dead. He said, "Leave your girls at home and get to the hospital as quickly as you can." Deep down, I knew.

Only a few miles from our home, Matt was being extricated from his car by the fire department. He wasn't breathing and he did not have a pulse. They tried to revive him.

With my husband driving I begged and pleaded with God all the way to the Hospital. My child was hurt, every parent's worst nightmare. We were taken to my son by the ER staff. CPR was being performed. There were so many people trying to save Matt. His color was bad. After looking at him I knew he wouldn't survive this. I announced to everyone in the room, "I know my son is dying but can you please work on him a few more minutes!" I went to Matt's side and encouraged him to fight. I told him he could do it, but there was nothing in his eyes. I could not believe this was happening. Through my tears I told Matt that I was not angry. That I knew it was an accident and that he did not intend for this to happen. I told him he was a great son and that I would love him forever.

The room suddenly became very quiet and then the time of my son's death was called. I held Matt and told him how much I loved him. I cleaned him, gave him a kiss and said goodbye. I was forced to leave him knowing he would be all alone. I had to get home to Elise, Alexa and Mea.

At times, I believe Matt was taken from us to serve a greater good. There have been many signs that would suggest this. Matt's bible was found in his locker, earmarked to Psalms 23. His license plate number was 523 KPZ. Matt died on May 23rd and was always saying "k peace."

The summer before Matt's death, my husband, some friends and Matt went golfing at Laural View Golf Course in Hamden. They were on the 4th hole and Matt could not find his golf ball. They searched around the green only to find it was in the hole. He had scored an eagle! Matt reacted by flapping his arms like an eagle while he "flew" around the green. Last summer my husband returned to Laural View for another round. While playing the 4th hole of the course with Matt on his mind, he noticed a cloud in the sky which resembled an eagle.

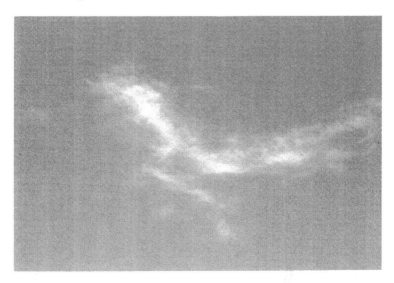

I myself had a strange feeling for months before Matt's accident. Although I was working full time, raising four children, and taking care of our home, I felt the need to do more. I thought about volunteering at the food bank or helping out somehow. I couldn't connect with any particular charity at the time, and now I know why.

Matt put in his yearbook that he wanted to make a difference. After his death, I started Matt Picciuto Scholarship Fund. Last year, we held The Slow Down for Matt Walk and drew over 1000 participants. We raised over $33,000 in his name. This year, I established Matt's Mission Fund and we expanded the walk to include a 5K road race. All money raised will be used to help students from North Branford, providing relief to students and their families. The events honor Matt's memory, increase awareness that encourages people to slow down and to drive safe, while supporting Matt's Mission Fund. Matt wanted to make a difference, and he is.

–Lynn Riodan
North Branford

Psalm 23
A psalm of David.

The LORD is my shepherd, I shall not be in want.

He makes me lie down in green pastures,

   he leads me beside quiet waters,

He restores my soul.

He guides me in paths of righteousness

for his name's sake.

Even though I walk

   through the valley of the shadow of death, [a]

   I will fear no evil,

   for you are with me;

   your rod and your staff,

   they comfort me.

You prepare a table before me

   in the presence of my enemies.

   You anoint my head with oil;

my cup overflows.

Surely goodness and love will follow me

all the days of my life,

and I will dwell in the house of the LORD

forever.

A Gifted Dream

This happened nine years ago, but I can still remember every detail as plain as day. My mother was gravely ill and in the hospital. After I finished my shift at work, I went home and cooked dinner. Then, I went directly to the hospital to see my mother.

I stayed with her for quite some time. Sadly, there was no improvement in her condition and she did not even know that I was there. The morphine drip continued to keep her from pain as she slept peacefully. I kissed her on the cheek and returned home.

That night I had a dream. In the dream someone rang my doorbell. When I answered the door there was man standing there and a black limousine in my driveway. He motioned me to get in and go for a ride with him. Frighten, I say no. He turned and began walking down the steps. I suddenly changed my mind and decided to go along with him.

The driver was also a man, but I did not see his face as he never turned around. I remember saying that my mother could not die. I loved her so much and if she died I would have no one! I received no answer. No reply to my plea. As soon as the limousine began driving away I woke up.

Two days later, my mother passed away. The hospital Chaplin came to bless her. I talked to him about my dream. He told me that it was a gifted dream, and that angels had come to prepare me for my mother's death.

When she passed, she had a look of peace, and a tear in her eye. She was finally at rest. There is not a day that goes by that I don't cry for her. I miss her, but I also know that she is in Heaven now. And, I do believe that angels are always by our side.

– *Maria Vazquez*
New Haven

In Life and In Death

It was February 14, 2007. Here is was Valentine's Day, and I was driving home from work in a snow storm! The Boston Post Road was at a standstill so I foolishly turned off onto a back road.

As the snow intensified, my wipers failed. I lost control of my car and plowed through a wooden fence into someone's front yard and then directly into a tree. When I became conscience I was bleeding from my forehead. Then, I remember seeing my boyfriend Jim hovering over me. Directly behind him was a woman dressed in all white with a sun-like glow radiating from her. I soon recognized her. It was Joanne, my boyfriend's sister. She had died from cancer more than a year prior.

Her hand was on Jim's shoulder and she shook her head. I tried to tell Jim that she was there, but he wouldn't listen.

A week after the accident I visited Joanne's gravesite. I thought at the time that she had come that night for me. I prayed for an answer, the truth as to what had happened and why. On March 8th I received my answer. Jim had been found unresponsive. He was immediately hospitalized.

As I knelt beside him in his hospital bed holding the rosary, I felt something or someone in the room. Jim blinked his eyes and cried. I felt a cold chill come upon me. Soon after, Jim passed away.

I now know that Joanne came to prepare me that night of the accident, not for my death, but for Jims. The officer who arrived at the scene told me that I must have had an angel on my shoulder for surviving such a tragic crash. He was right. I know that there was also an angel that night preparing me for what lied ahead.

Joanne knew her brother would be joining her in Heaven. Ironically, they both died from inoperable brain cancer. I firmly believe in angels and know that they are here for us in life and in death.

– Patricia Dimassa-Rida
West Haven

A Robin Brings Daily Joy

My story begins three years ago when my husband was sick with cancer. He had been receiving treatments for several months, but was not improving. At the same time, my 86-year-old mother was living with us and she was diagnosed with Alzheimer's disease. My mother's sister was in a nursing home in Cheshire, and my older sister was very ill and in and out of the hospital. Needless to say, I was feeling very helpless and hopeless.

One day in May 2007, I returned home from a hospital visit with my husband. I felt a strong urge to go to my kitchen sink. I looked out the window above the sink which overlooks my backyard. The first thing I saw was this beautiful red-breasted robin perched on a branch that had fallen off a tree. There was something about this bird that held my attention for quite a while. A feeling of relief came over me, but I wasn't sure why. I lifted up the window and continued to stare out at the bird. He did not fly away. Instead he lifted his head and stared at me. There were other birds flying back and forth in different areas of my back yard from tree to tree, but this robin did not move. It started to get dark so I left the window and tended to my mother.

The following day when I returned home from the hospital, I was again drawn to the kitchen window. There was the red-breasted robin perched on the fallen branch. As soon as I turned the faucet on and the sound of running water could be heard, he lifted up his head and stared at me. I had a feeling that this was the same bird from the day before. His mannerisms were identical to the way he acted the day before. This scenario became a daily event in the spring and summer of 2007. Each day I would rush home just to see if he was still there. He was! I felt so much joy in my spirit because this little creature was becoming a true friend.

In early June, my husband was transferred to Hospice. He died on June 24. Over the following months that little bird continued to be a bright spot in my life. Around October, as the weather became colder, he was gone. In December my older sister passed away, and my mother's sister passed in February 2008. I longed for my robin friend during that time of sorrow, and continued to look out the window daily.

A few months had passed. It was now May and I looked out the window around 6 p.m., as I had continued to do throughout the long winter months. There he was, perched upon another branch that had fallen in my back yard! I turned the faucet on and let the water run. He then lifted his head very high, stretching his neck toward the window. My heart immediately filled with joy at the sight of my robin friend. I went outside and stood on the deck for seemingly hours just staring at this little friend of mine who made me feel so happy. As a person of great faith, I knew that God had sent an angel to be with me. It was no coincidence that he came at the same time every day and now for the second year. He continued to come every day until cold weather set in.

In February of 2009, through some kind of divine intervention, I found myself in touch with a special childhood friend. He was my first sweetheart and I had not seen or spoken to him in 49 years. I immediately thought that God knew I was going to need someone special in my life at that time. Only three weeks after I started communicating with my old friend, my mother was hospitalized.

During her hospital stay, he called me daily to encourage me and minister to me with messages from God. I found comfort in his phones calls, text messages and emails. He lived on the West Coast and I lived on the East Coast, but our daily contact kept us connected. Sadly, in March, my mother passed away. My long distant friend continued to be a great comfort to me. And, after burying my mother in West Virginia, I returned home to find my angel bird in my backyard.

Throughout the spring and summer of 2009, my angel bird continued to come on a daily basis. However, now I also noticed doves flying about in my trees. I had not seen any doves before this time. At the end of the summer I took a trip to Seattle to reunite with my childhood friend. Upon returning home, my angel bird was gone. For weeks I looked out the window only to find an empty yard.

It was then that I received a clear message in my spirit. That message was that God had replaced one angel with another. My special childhood friend who I have now grown very close to had become that angel. God always knows what, when and who we need. I am truly blessed to have had these angels in my life.

– *Patricia Younger*
Hamden

It is better, much better, to have wisdom and knowledge than gold and silver.
—Prov. 16:16

An Angel in a Wheelchair

I was receiving a course of treatment for prostate cancer at the Father McGivney Cancer Center at St. Raphael's Hospital in New Haven. My treatment schedule was five days a week at 8 a.m. each morning.

On one snowy morning in February 2008, I was returning to my parked car after a treatment. It was then that I heard a woman's voice call out, "Mister, mister!" I turned around and saw a young woman in a motorized chair stuck in about 4 inches of snow. I checked for traffic, crossed the street, lifted her chair back to the sidewalk, and made sure she could proceed.

After I returned to my car I turned around to be sure she was alright. She was gone. There was no sign of her anywhere and no tracks in the snow.

I believe God sent this angel in a wheelchair to perhaps test my kindness on earth. And, although I could have easily continued to my car without helping her, in my heart I knew I had to assist her. Nine weeks later my cancer was in remission and as of today there is no indication that it has returned.

– *Peter Palmieri*
Hamden

Trust in the Lord, with all your heart.
Never rely on what you think you know.
Remember the Lord in everything you do,
and He will show you the way.
—Prov. 3:5-6

The Coin Collector

One beautiful Spring Saturday, my son Adam went to a 12-year-old friend's birthday party. It was in East Haven near the town beach. Many activities were planned including rollerblading. When we arrived, I realized that the children were not going to be as supervised as I would have liked, but I let him attend anyway and hoped that he would be okay.

The first thing the boys decided to do was go walk the beach. When they got there they saw a man with a hat on. He was combing the beach using one of those electronic coin finders. Adam said the other boys thought he looked a little scary, but he didn't think so. Being 12-year-old boys they moved on quickly and decided it was time to put on their rollerblades and headed down the street. They were going up and down the many streets near the beach and crossing some busy intersections. It had now been quite a while since they had seen the man with the hat collecting coins.

The boys decided to head back toward the beach. They came to an intersection where the hedges blocked their view. Adam was first to approach the corner. When he passed the hedges, sure enough a car was coming. It was not going at a high speed as there was a stop sign at the corner, and the driver was just starting to accelerate. It was then that Adam skated out in front of the car. He turned toward the car, landed on the hood, and then was thrown off and back about twenty feet.

An ambulance was called and came to the scene. When they arrived, they could not believe how little Adam was hurt.

He only had a bruised knee. They called us immediately, but assured us that he was fine.

After we picked him up and took him home I asked Adam what he remembered about the accident. He said that right after the car hit him he didn't remember anything until he opened his eyes. Then he was in the arms and lap of the man from the beach, the man with the hat and the coin finder. The next thing he remembered was the EMT's checking him.

The next day I asked some of his friends if they saw the man holding Adam at the scene of the accident. None of them did.

My father died when I was pregnant with Adam and I truly felt that this was a divine intervention. It was either Adam's own guardian angel or an intervention prompted by his grandfather. I believe what Adam told me and what he saw that day, and I know he was and still is protected by angels.

– Roseann Della Ventura
Hamden

My Angel Alerts Me

I am a 69-year-old diabetic. There were a few times when I was woken from a sound sleep. I say woken because I felt as if someone was poking me to wake up. It was on those nights that my sugar level was extremely low. Because I woke up, I had time to get orange juice and bring my levels to normal again.

There have been other times when my sugar is low and I just have a feeling to test my levels. Sure enough my sugar level is low and I have enough time to bring it back to normal.

I believe that my guardian angel watches over me at all times, and she alerts me when I am in danger. I thank God for angels and know in my heart that I am never alone.

– *Teresa Izzo*
East Haven

Life isn't about finding yourself.
Life is about creating yourself.
—Unknown

An Angel Encounter on I-95

It was a cool crisp November morning in 2005 on my way to work. It was the day I survived a near-fatal car accident. My angel encounter was in the midst of the worst of the accidents' violence. I will not go into any specific details about the accident itself because I cannot remember those details. I was unconscious before I was thrown out of the car. But I do remember the angels, and perhaps that is the most important thing.

Three of them came to me when my body went through glass out of my rapidly and violently rolling-over SUV. Witnesses said it was so horrible it seems to be unreal. Some thought it must have been a movie scene being filmed! They wondered if maybe this was just a stunt doll being propelled out of the car flying across all lanes of the highway landing on her head on the other side of the road. But it was me doing that flying! And the angels were flying with me, as I later recalled.

A state trooper came to visit me at the hospital when I was beginning to improve. I was aware at this point that my survival from this accident was nothing short of a miracle. This particular trooper was the first on the scene at the accident. He found no signs of life and so resuscitated me. The trooper told me that what was so amazing was that my body landed on a little patch of ground, though everything else in the whole area of the accident was asphalt and metal, including a metal electrical transformer, metal railings and, of course, the unyielding highway.

But the trooper said that my body was in the only place that would have allowed any possibility for me to make it. This made me think about what love, protection, and comfort I must have been given on that day, the day that changed my life. Then I remembered the angels who put my body in that one safe spot along the highway: There were three brunette angels, no wings, but they were sure able to fly. They had a beautiful white light all around them and it was tinged with a golden aura.

Though I realize that angels don't have to have bodies, these angels appeared to me in a kind of human form, and one looked at me with eyes of such kindness and beauty, she smiled at me, too. Her eyes seemed to penetrate my being, there was a glow in them that was clearly not human, and it was divine. The angel told me: "we are helping you, we are taking you to safety, do not be afraid." I cry as I write this because I am experiencing pure joy at the memory of this precious divine being, this light of God, giving me assurance and care and love.

The supervisor for the state troopers of which my first human hero was a part later told me that head injury victims in the kind of accident I was in almost never survive or that if live they function at a much lower level than prior to the injury. He said he rarely saw such a recovery as mine in his years out there on the highways in Connecticut. I told him I had special help and I believe it came from a Higher Power's band of angels. This guy didn't flinch when I said that, he appeared to nod his head in agreement.

I have come to believe that a lot of things have nothing to do with people per se, because something else is there when human powers cannot possibly come through, when human powers are not enough, though God knows there were many "earth angels" who helped me at the time of this accident and throughout my time recovering.

But I will never forget these darling angels from above who came to help me. I don't recall asking them to come, but I have now heard that angels just appear automatically when it is life-and-death. You don't have to ask. They never intrude but they do come when they are needed and I certainly needed them on that day in 2005.

I especially remember that one angel who looked at me and somehow communicated with me, though it was different from a human voice. But it was a voice, it was an energy. And she was all unconditional love, this angel. And the others took her guidance as to what do for me. This "lead" angel was on my right side holding me up. She had the other two angels positioned at my left side and underneath me. They then carried me to safety, to that one spot, that tiny spot on the highway that I went into with my head. In that moment I was given a love that I cannot define in human language and that is the love of God's angels. Love is all they know.

A couple of years after my accident, with my children in the car, one of them driving, we passed by that spot that I had been brought to by the Angels of Connecticut I-95. I felt a great vibration of light and warmth coming over me. I believe that those angels made it possible for me to return to my children and be their mother and now to be a grandmother to my daughter's little girl. The angels knew my time on this earth was not done. I love those angels forever. I hope to meet them again someday. I am sure I will, and it doesn't have to be on a highway.

– *Sarah Murray*
Branford

He will cover you with his feathers,
and under his wings you will find refuge;
his faithfulness will be your
shield and rampart.
–Psalm 91:4

My Realization, It Only Took 17 Years!

When does one know they have sat with or spoke to a deceased person, a spirit guide or an Angel? For me, it took about 17 years for the realization to actually set in. I always knew something "different" or should I say that something "special" happened when I was alone in my Nana and Pop-pop's den.

I could never get anyone to understand just what it was, not until the day we were celebrating their 60th wedding anniversary at the Branford VFW Hall in the spring of 1994. Displayed around the hall were several photos and albums of my grandparents' lives together. As I began looking through them, I saw her, the woman from my youth, the one I used to have milk and cookies with, the lady in the den, the one that always had the green afghan on, my dad's grandmother.

Throughout my youth my entire family never could understand who I spoke of when I would ask, "Who was the woman that lived at Nana's when we did?" or "Who was it that used to sleep in the den at Nana's?" Now here she was, in front of me, clear as day in the picture. I immediately called my father over to the table, showed him the picture of the woman wearing the white blouse with purple trim, slight tint of silver in her hair and blurted, "Dad, this is the lady who lived in Nana and Pop-pop's house when we did, you know the one I always talk about and you told me I didn't know, but here she is, this is her." The look on his face was one of pure amazement, mixed with a bit of shock. He immediately called over my aunt and uncle and a huge discussion ensued about what I had said. After a lengthy discussion they came to the realization, as I did, that I had encountered an Angel in the form of my great-grandmother. There could be no other explanation for she had passed on many years before my parents had even married or met. My memories were so vivid of her and our encounters!

My encounters with my Angel were wonderful. I remember them like they were yesterday, sitting together again. We were staying with my grandparents in Branford while our new house in North Haven was in the last phase of construction. Each afternoon I would head to the den, in the back of the house off of the dining room to visit "the lady". She was always so welcoming to me, with her bright smile. She lay upon the make shift bed with her green afghan covering her body from her waist to her feet. Next to the bed was a table that always had a plate of chocolate chip cookies and a glass of milk for me. I would sit in my Nana's rocking chair and tell the lady what had occurred throughout the day while I ate and drank. She would sit on the bed, smiling and nodding her head, as if I could say nothing wrong.

After realizing that I indeed had these encounters, I looked back at those days a little closer and realized a few things about the events with my Angel. I realized; she never spoke, never ate or drank, always smiled, always wore the same delicate white blouse, her hair always looked beautifully done, the green afghan always covered her, and I never saw her feet. Another thing I realized is that it was my secret, I tended to whisper if I heard anyone in the kitchen or dining room, which just happened to be the two closest rooms to the den.

It took many years for my family to believe that I spoke with my great-grandmother, because they knew she had passed on, however once I pointed out "the lady" I spoke with, they too realized that I spoke with an Angel, my great-grandmother. That was a wonderful realization. I hope anyone who has an Angel encounter has others who believe their stories.

– *Stephanie Palmieri*
Cheshire

I saw the angel in the marble and carved until I set him free.
—Michelangelo

True and Everlasting Love

I was a 19-year-old girl, very shy and feeling unloved. I felt like I was heading in the wrong direction and wanted more from life. It was then that I started going to church every morning before heading to work. I prayed and prayed that I would find the right path to travel, and to find someone to love. This went on for several weeks.

One morning when I was praying, I heard a voice say that everything was going to be alright. Several months later I met Lee.

I was getting my car fixed at my Uncle Fergie's garage when my friend Andy suggested I take ride down to the diner. He wanted to introduce me to someone. Well Lee walked out the door, stood there with his hands on his hips and his head held high. I thought he looked too big for his britches and I didn't want to meet him.

A couple of weeks went by and I saw him at my uncle's garage again. We spoke briefly and I saw him a few more times at the garage after that.

It was Christmas Eve and I went to the garage to wish my uncle a Merry Christmas. Lee was there. He asked me to go out with him. I told him I was going to church with my parents. To my surprise, he asked if he could come along with me. That was our first date, going to church together.

On New Year's Day, he took me to dinner at his sister's house. On the way home, he stopped his car on the side of the road and asked if he could kiss me. I said yes. That kiss made me feel like I was in Heaven! The next day when I went to work, I felt like I was walking on a cloud. I was so very happy and excited, my heart was still racing. All of a sudden, I heard "You're Just in Love" by Perry Como and the Fontane Sisters. Right then I knew I had fallen in love with Lee. He was a perfect gentleman and always kept his word.

On January 12, Lee asked me to marry him and I said yes! When I told my family and friends, they said I was crazy because he was 15 years older than me, he was a truck driver, and we had only dated for two weeks. Despite their opinions, I knew in my heart that he was the only man for me.

We were married on January 31, only five weeks after we began dating. We had four children, 11 grandchildren and were married 51 years and 9 months before God called Lee home to Heaven.

It was October 18, 2009 and the doctor told us that Lee's condition had gotten a lot worse and that he only had a short time to live. Lee looked at me, took my hand, gave me a wink and a small smile. He told me that he was ready to go home and see his deceased family members, but if there is any possible way, he would send me a message. Two weeks later Lee passed away.

I had a hard time dealing with his death. I cried a lot. I knew he was better off where he was but I missed him so much. It was New Year's Eve when I had a dream that my whole family was at my home. We were decorating and completing projects when I heard a loud noise in my grandson's room. I went in and suddenly something lifted me up and carried me from room to room. I felt so happy and all I could say was, "He's here. Lee is here." The next morning when I woke up, I felt like my spirits were lifted and I was happy again.

As time went on, there was another night that I was again missing him and crying so hard. I asked Lee over and over if we would be together when my time came and I passed on. It seemed like hours before I finally fell asleep. Then I woke up out of a sound sleep to hear a voice in my head saying, "My baby, my love." At that very moment I felt relieved and happier. The next day I kept humming a song, and I don't normally hum. I realized it was the same song that I heard when I fell in love with Lee, it was "You're Just in Love."

Looking back over my life, I think it all started with my going to church and praying for someone to love. And, then our first date was in church. I know angels are with us and they have answered my prayers in many ways.

– *Sylvia Belomizi*
(Wife of Lee Belomizi)
Northford

Faith is taking the first step even when you don't see the whole staircase.
—Martin Luther King, Jr.

Hail Mary, Full of Grace

I grew up on Long Island, New York. I had a hardworking father and four brothers. We were religious, but by no means a devout Catholics.

When I was 11, I remember walking down the street and a boy about 4 years older than I stopped me. Out of nowhere, he asked me what I knew about Jesus Christ. We talked in detail about Jesus at the time, and then I continued on my way.

My life was pleasantly average I would say. I met the woman of my dreams at an early age. Within minutes of meeting her, I fell in love and have been in love ever since. We've been happily married for 55 years now. We proudly have three children and five grandchildren.

In 1978 I had the opportunity to visit Israel. I walked where Jesus was born, raised, and died on the cross. I carried a bible with me and recorded my trip as I connected to this Holy region.

A few years ago, my son purchased a car that was going to be rebuilt. The man working on the car invited me to attend a cenacle, a gathering of people devoting prayer and honor to the Virgin Mary. I attended three times.

About a month later, I was given a spiritual gift. I was at my home in Madison, it was 5 p.m. and the sun was just setting in the west, which is located behind my shed. I noticed an image on my shed. I ran inside and grabbed my camera.

I had to capture this amazing image, and now I share it with you.

I see Virgin Mary in prayer around what seems like a triangle, as do many other people I have shared this with. There are other circles of light around and below the image. I believe they are the angels who surround her.

I am blessed to have witnessed this, to have captured it on film. And, now I am thankful to be able to share it with you.

– *Ned Macomb*
Madison

The Skeleton Key

It was a windy day in March 1979 and I was 8-months pregnant with my second child. I wanted my children to have their own room so I decided to convert my living room into a bedroom. Remodeling required the purchase of new carpeting. When the carpet was delivered, I let the drivers in through my front door. This was an old door that required a special key. It looked like a skeleton key, only very small and old.

After the installation was complete, I went to close the door. The key was missing. I began to scour the floor and surrounding area near the door. It was nowhere! The room was just a small front hall with a cedar closet in it. It couldn't have gone far, but I didn't see it anywhere. I finally called my father who was with me the entire time the carpet was being installed. He helped me look. Together, we still couldn't find it.

Over the next three years we did some remodeling work in that front hall. This included adding a cabinet to store towels and sheets. One day I went to the front hall to get sheets for my bed. I froze. I could not believe my eyes. There it was – the skeleton key that had been missing for three years! I called my father down to show him. The key was back, so shiny right on the rug in front of us.

For three years, I had to use a letter opener to open that door. For three years, I prayed to find that key. I don't know how, but I believe an angel brought that key back to me. Perhaps it was to prevent one of the children from getting hurt. I am not sure. What I do know is that angels are real. We may not be able to see them, but they are there for each and every one of us.

To this very day, that key is still in the door!

– *Terry Marchitto*
East Haven

Heartfelt Message from Mom

My mom passed away 13 years ago at the age of 60. She was a strong woman that lived for her children and never really had a chance to enjoy a good life. My mother was diagnosed with lung cancer and within a short time it took her life. My brothers, sisters and I did all we could to keep her home in her own apartment as long as possible. Eventually she needed more care and money was running out so she came to live with me and my family during the last months of her life.

Spending time with someone you love and cherish, knowing you will soon say goodbye, is the hardest thing to do. My mom and I were very close. At night we would talk about many things, and I can remember asking my mother to please send me some kind of sign so I would know she was okay.

Many years had passed since her death, and in March 2009 I had to have a hysterectomy. I had complications and was very scared. I found myself wishing that my mom was here to be with me and comfort me. I could not even get out of bed as it was too painful. During this time, I slept in our spare room, which was where my mom stayed during her final days.

My husband encouraged me one day to come downstairs and have breakfast. So I made my way slowly downstairs. When I entered the kitchen, my husband asked, "What is that sticking out of your shirt?" I put my hand on my chest and felt something. It was my mom's heart-shaped crystal. She had two heart-shaped crystal keepsakes that I kept beside my bed in my bedroom. They were given to her on her last birthday by co-workers and they had her name and birth date engraved on them. But, I was not even in our bedroom that morning! I was so confused and happy at the same time. I believe that was a message from my mom. She was with me and this was a sign from her.

That same year on mother's birthday in May, I was in my driveway getting into my car when I saw a glare on the ground by the driver's side. There in my driveway was a beautiful angel pin and she was holding a star. In the star was a pearl, my birthstone. I am a collector of angels and my mother knew that. Again, I believe that she way letting me know that she is here and always will be with me and that she is happy now.

– *Toni Ann McKane*
West Haven

Gift on the Window Sill

I have always believed in angels. I have two little angels in a box on the window sill of my picture window where I sit and pray. Every morning, along with my usual inspirational readings, I touch them and ask them to watch over me.

I have recently been diagnosed with cancer in my lymph nodes and I ask my angels for additional healing. One morning I was preparing for my daily meditation routine, and as I reached out to touch one of the angels, a gold medal with a picture of an angel (about the size of a quarter) was in the box next to one of the angels.

I was a little stunned at first. I asked my husband if he put it there. He said no.

The only other medal I've seen like this one was a tarnished one that I had kept in my car for years. I then checked my car and the tarnished one was still there.

I believe this medal was a gift from an angel – one who came to bless me and let me know that my prayers are being heard.

– *Valerie Vasseur*
North Haven

There are two ways to live your life. One is as though nothing is a miracle. The other is as though everything is a miracle.
–Albert Einstein

Angels Never Leave You Flat

I was on my way to work in my new 1990 Eagle. It was early morning and all was quiet as I traveled along Lake Quonnipaug in North Guilford. As I approached the most dangerous turn on Route 77 I got a flat in the right rear tire. It was fiercely raining. I pulled over to safety. Since my car was new I did not know where all the gear was to change the tire. At the time, I didn't have a cell phone and couldn't call for roadside assistance. My only options were to walk nearly a mile in the rain back to my house, or knock on someone's door. I hesitated since it was only 7:30 in the morning.

While pondering over what I should do I heard a tap on my side window. There, standing in the rain, was a young gentleman in raingear offering to change my flat. He quickly went to the back of my car as if he knew just where to find all the tools then proceeded to fix my flat. He had parked his red van behind my car for protection and gave me an umbrella while I stood in the rain watching him.

After he finished I was so grateful that I wanted him to write his name and address down for me. He declined and said it was not necessary. I returned his umbrella and he took off in his van. I was still in a daze as to what had taken place as I continued on my way to work. For weeks after, I looked for the red van while on my way to work. I looked on the road, in driveways, but it was never seen again. I believe that man was an angel who came to my rescue that day.

Nearly ten years later, I was traveling on the College Street Bridge in New Haven. Before turning to get on the interstate, my rear right tire went flat. Again it was raining heavily, only this time it was dark and the visibility was poor. It was about 9:30 p.m. and the streets were very deserted. Since I had just left work, I had all the receipts from that day in my briefcase. I now carried a cell phone, but before I could call for assistance there was a tap at my window. A man soaking wet from the rain was there offering to change my tire.

I must admit that I was a little taken back at his sudden appearance and his immediate response to assist me. I kept the window shut as I talked to him. However, his face seemed so sincere that I pushed the briefcase under the seat and opened the door to accept his help. I was driving a Ford Explorer and the extra tire was hidden under the back. I opened the back hatch giving both of us protection from the rain. He seemed to know exactly what to do. He was gentle and worked very quickly changing the tire and then organizing everything back into place in my trunk.

When he finished, he told me to have a good evening and stay dry then started walking away. I called to him, fishing in my pocket for money to offer him which he took reluctantly. Then he walked off into the darkness. I did not get his name, but I was very thankful for his appearance.

God must know that I don't know how to change a tire, so He sends angels to help me when I'm stranded and I am forever thankful.

– Vincent J. Farricielli
Orange

Part 3
Finding Inner-Peace

*Peace. It does not mean to be in a place where
there is no noise, trouble or hard work.
It means to be in the midst of those things
and still be calm in your heart.
—Unknown*

Meditations

The mind is constantly jumping from one thing to another. Where to go? What to do? Work, cook, clean! Too much of today's society involves running from one place to another. An easy way to calm your mind is through meditation. It creates a blank page in your mind allowing you to feel less stressed and more connected spiritually.

It is simple to do. All you need is a quiet place and a few minutes. You can sit on the floor, in a chair, or lay down. However you are comfortable is fine. Be sure to turn your phone off. If you'd like, you can light a candle or incense before you begin. Meditate with a friend by taking turns reading, or use a tape-recorder to record your own voice.

Listed below are a couple of my favorite meditations.

Mind-Clearing

Make yourself comfortable in a quiet area.
Close your eyes and focus on your breathing.
When you inhale, breathe in peace.
When you exhale, breathe out stress.
If any thoughts enter your mind, push them aside.
Now breathe in love, and breathe out hate.
Feel your body slowing. Your heart rate begins to regulate.
Continue by breathing in Hope, and breathing out Doubt.
Feel your shoulders becoming lighter with each exhale.
Breathe in relaxation, and breathe out tension.
Repeat this as long as you'd like until you feel at peace.
When you have finished this meditation, open your eyes.
You will feel calm and refreshed.

Gounding

Make yourself comfortable in a quiet area.

Close your eyes. Breathe slowly as you relax your body.

Focus your attention on your feet. Then slowly move your awareness up your body.

Relax your calves, thighs, hips, torso, arms, shoulders, neck, and head.

Continue breathing slowly. In and out.

Now imagine that you are surrounded by a white light. Let it glow around your entire being.

Inhale this light and allow it to fill your body.

Continue to inhale the light. As you exhale, release any tension you feel in your body.

Breathe in the light. Exhale the tension.

Now, picture tiny roots growing out of the soles of your feet and the base of your spine.

Feel them growing as they extend all the way down into the earth beneath you.

Continue breathing in light and exhaling tension as these roots begin to take hold, securing you to the center of the earth. Like the roots of a tree you are connected to the earth.

Imagine now that you can breathe through your roots.

Like liquid through a straw, draw the energy of the earth up through these roots.

Let the energy fill your heart and entire body.

Now bring your attention to the top of your head.

Imagine a small circle of light opening above you.

Rays of light begin to emerge. They stretch up into the sky, in the heavens above.

The rays connect you to the sun, the stars and planets, and the entire universe.

As you inhale, breathe in the energy of the heavens. Allow this energy to come down through the top of your head and fill your entire body.

Now breathe in both the energies. Up from the earth, down from the heavens.

Allow these two energies to fill your heart and your entire body.

Up from the earth, down from the heavens.

You are now securely anchored between Heaven and Earth.

When you are ready, you can become aware of your body, of your surroundings.

Feel your breath rise and fall. Feel your heartbeat.

Slowly, in your own time, open your eyes.

Journaling

I remember my very first journal entry. A student at the time, my instructor suggested we begin keeping a journal. I wrote the date and then jotted down *I have nothing to write about.* That was several years ago. Now when I journal, it is sometimes 10 pages long!

When you put something in writing, it becomes real. Think about legal documents, contracts, even texting someone. So praying, asking for our needs and goals to be fulfilled, all that we desire can be put into writing as well. And so it becomes real.

Find a place that is quiet. Yes, it is possible to tune out the world. Meditate before you begin or simply clear your mind by breathing in peace and breathing out stress for a few minutes. Then, write whatever you are feeling at the moment. Be sure to write the day, date, time, and place. You can even note the weather and how you are feeling at the moment. You can address your entries specifically to your angels if you would like.

You can begin by asking a question. For example, *Dear Angels, What is my life's purpose?* Then just start writing. Perhaps you will write about your current situation, or a past relationship. Whatever is on your mind, write it down. You can write anything you want. It's *your* journal.

Sometimes when life seems uncontrollable, writing it down puts things into perspective. This is a good way to set life goals. Remember, getting from one place to another requires a road map. Setting goals is like planning your route, taking one step at a time as you travel your life's path.

If there is something bothering you that you would like to get rid of, write it down. Just getting it out of your head and onto paper will help to release it. Some people will even burn or shred what they have written in order to release it.

Remember also that a positive attitude equals positive results. Be thankful for all that you do have. Stay focused on what makes you happy within your heart. Even if there are 99 negative things happening in your life, focus on the one positive. Someone told me once that you have 11 seconds to release a negative thought. I like that and use it whenever I need to.

May there always be an angel by your side.

Made in the USA
Charleston, SC
12 May 2011